Reading Comprehension

Grade 4

Recently, many students have been taught to read using such "no-fail" techniques as sight reading, picture reading, and whole language.

While it is probable that some students responded well to some of these new techniques, it is also likely that many others were unable to learn to read using these alternative methods. It is for these students that the *Basics First* books were created.

The back-to-basics method is tried and true. It provides students with an approach they can use to learn all of the skills needed for a particular subject. Many of these fundamental techniques may even have helped you learn to read when you were a child!

To help students learn to comprehend what they read, this *Basics First* book offers an interesting fact- or fiction-based story on every other page. Each narrative has been written so that a student at a fourth-grade level can read it successfully. After each story, there are activities that will help students practice the following skills: locating the main idea, reading for details, putting events in order, following directions, determining the cause and the effect of an action, recognizing similarities and differences, analyzing characters, predicting outcomes, drawing inferences, and much more. The carefully thought-out questions help a student learn to think, respond, create, imagine, and even do research to learn more about a subject.

You will be thrilled when the students using this book want to read more as they begin to better understand what they are reading. They will also learn to question and will develop higher-level thinking skills that are necessary in so many important aspects in life. Most of all, this book will help students recognize reading as an enjoyable way to spend their time.

The White House Gang

Name _____

The White House is the large house in which our president lives. Can you imagine living there? The six children of one president thought it was great fun! Theodore Roosevelt, our 26th president, moved into the White House with his wife, four boys, and two girls. The Roosevelt children loved playing with each other and their father. Some people called these children "the White House gang" because of the mischief they got into.

The Roosevelt children had many pets including an enormous blue parrot named Eli. They also kept a bear, a lizard, a one-legged rooster, a barn owl, a rabbit, a pig, and a pony. One time, one of Roosevelt's sons rode the pony upstairs to see his sick brother. Another time, the children spit paper balls at a picture of President Andrew Jackson. They also sent their father a note saying they had gone to war with the White House. In fun, their father asked for peace through his war department. The Roosevelt children got into much mischief while they lived in the White House.

---

1. Put a √ in front of the main idea of this story.

   ___ **The president's children had many unusual pets.**

   ___ **President Roosevelt loved his mischief-making children.**

   ___ **One of Roosevelt's sons rode a pony upstairs to see his sick brother.**

   ___ **Most presidents have children.**

   ___ **The Roosevelt children had fun while living in the White House.**

   ___ **Everyone wants to live in the White House.**

2. Circle the correct sentence.

   The White House gang got into mischief in the White House.

   The White House gang robbed banks and were sent to jail.

2

FS-30023 Reading Comprehension

The White House Gang

Name _____

3. In your own words, write what "mischief" means? _____

_____

4. Tell about some mischievous things the Roosevelt children did in the White House.

_____

_____

_____

5. In complete sentences, explain what you think about the mischief the children created.

_____

_____

6. Make an outline of the story on a separate sheet of paper. Be sure to include the main idea in the outline.

7. Write the kinds of pets the Roosevelt children had. _____

_____

8. Write which of these pets you would want and why. _____

_____

_____

9. What did President Roosevelt do when his children sent him a note saying they had gone to war with the White House?_____

_____

10. Write the names of three other U.S. Presidents. _____

_____

11. On the back of this page, draw a picture of you and a pet standing next to the White House.

12. On page 2, color the horse brown, the pig pink, the parrot blue, and the rooster red.

Try This!
- What kind of pet would you take to live in the White House? Why?
- Use a reference book to find out about other children who lived in the White House. Write a two-paragraph story about them.

3

Living With Gorillas

Name _____

Dian Fossey was born in California in 1932. Although she only lived to be 53, Fossey was famous around the world when she died. Was she an actress? Was she a singer? Believe it or not, Dian Fossey was famous for studying mountain gorillas!

Before Fossey became interested in gorillas, she spent her time in college learning to help people. After working for several years, Fossey one day read a book about mountain gorillas. She was so excited that she borrowed money to go to Africa to see them!

While she was in Africa, Fossey had a stroke of good luck. She met a man named Louis Leakey, a well-respected scientist. Leakey wanted someone to study the mountain gorillas that lived in a country called Rwanda. Rwanda is located in east-central Africa. Leakey asked Dian Fossey to take that job. Fossey happily accepted.

Fossey studied gorillas for almost 18 years. She got very close to the animals, watching them for hours at a time, taking notes, and copying their sounds and habits. She named many of the gorillas, and after a while, she became their trusted friend.

Fossey soon found that hunters were killing the gorillas. After some of her favorites were killed, Fossey realized that the gorillas were in danger of dying out. Protecting them became her goal. Dian Fossey wanted people to know about the gorillas she loved, so she wrote a book, *Gorillas in the Mist*. The book was turned into a movie three years after she died. Fossey taught the world about mountain gorillas and worked hard to save them.

---

1. Circle the main idea of this story.

   Dian Fossey was a famous person when she died.

   Gorillas are in danger of dying out.

   The book, *Gorillas in the Mist*, was turned into a movie.

   Dian Fossey studied and taught other people about mountain gorillas.

   Louis Leakey asked Dian Fossey to study mountain gorillas in Rwanda.

FS-30023 Reading Comprehension

Name _____

2. What did Fossey do to teach other people about mountain gorillas? _____
_____

3. Circle the method Fossey used to learn about the gorillas.

   She watched them with field glasses and took notes.

   She copied their habits and sounds.

   She read books and watched movies about mountain gorillas.

4. After living among the gorillas for a short while, Fossey learned something that worried her. What was it? _____

5. Dian Fossey first became interested in mountain gorillas after she

   ___ **visited Africa and met Louis Leakey.**

   ___ **saw a movie called "Gorillas in the Mist."**

   ___ **read a book about them.**

6. Draw a box around the main idea in the story.

7. Write two things you learned about Dian Fossey in this story. _____
_____

_____

8. Write three facts about the animals the story tells about.

   1) _____

   2) _____

   3) _____

9. Write a new title for this story. Write why you chose the new name.

_____

_____

Try This!

• Go to the library and find out about a woman named Jane Goodall, who studied a different kind of ape—a chimpanzee. How were the lives of these two women similar? How were they different?

• Pretend you are Dian Fossey writing in your journal at the end of the day. Write about what you did today. Be sure to include what you saw happening and how you felt.

Did You Know That?

Name _____

What do you know about our presidents? Maybe you think they are all boring. If you think about it, though, everyone is interesting in some way. Are all of your friends the same size? Probably not. Well, presidents come in all sizes, too. James Madison, our fourth president, was the shortest president we have had so far. He was 5-feet-4-inches tall. Six-foot-four-inch Abraham Lincoln was the tallest, and he was also very thin. Lincoln was our 16th president. William Howard Taft, our 27th president, was the heaviest. He weighed more than 300 pounds and even got stuck in the White House bathtub the first time he used it! He had a bigger tub put in the White House soon after.

Do you take baths or showers? What would you do to keep clean if you had neither a bathtub nor a shower in your home? There were no showers or bathtubs in the White House during its first 50 years! Millard Fillmore, the 13th president, put the first bathtub in the White House after he became president in 1850!

Do you think of all presidents as old? Some presidents are old when they are elected, but others are young. Ronald Reagan, the oldest president to be elected, was 69 when he was elected our 40th president. He served as president for 8 years. How old did that make him when he left office? The youngest man to become president was 42-year-old Teddy Roosevelt, who became our 26th president. John F. Kennedy was also a young president. He was 43 when he was elected our 35th president in 1960. Both of these men brought young children to the White House. Teddy Roosevelt's children had a pony named Algonquin, and John Kennedy's children had a pony named Macaroni! These are just a few fun presidential facts. Where might you find more?

_____

1. List your two favorite facts about presidents. _____

   _____

   _____

2. Who was the youngest president? How old was he when he became president?

   _____

3. With a blue pencil or crayon, underline each presidential fact that has to do with size.

FS-30023 Reading Comprehension

Name _____

4. How many presidents had details that told about size? _____

5. Put a red circle around each sentence in the story that tells about a young president. How many did you circle? _____

6. Put a green circle around each sentence that tells about a young president's family pets. How many did you circle? _____

7. Match each president's name to the correct fact.

   _____ Abraham Lincoln   _____ Teddy Roosevelt   _____ William Taft

   a. tallest   b. oldest   c. heaviest   d. youngest

8. How many presidents are known for something about bathtubs? _____

9. Write the bathtub facts on these lines. _____

   _____

   _____

10. Name three details that were the same for Teddy Roosevelt and John Kennedy.

   _____

   _____

   _____

11. What details tell you they were also different in some ways? _____

   _____

   _____

   _____

12. Who was the shortest president? _____

13. How tall was the shortest president? _____

14. How tall was the tallest president? _____

15. Who was the tallest president? _____

16. Find a newspaper article about our current president. On the back of this page, write three facts about the article that interest you.

Try This! Pick a president and research facts about him at the library. Choose five of the most interesting details about his life and write a story about him.

Daddy Who?

Name _____

Maybe you have seen this creature, carefully making its way across your kitchen floor on its long legs. Someone may have told you about an old legend that says it is bad luck to kill one of these creatures. Is it a spider? An insect? Actually, a daddy longlegs is neither, although it does belong to the same family as spiders.

You may not feel like picking up a daddy longlegs from the floor with your bare hands, but you certainly could if you wanted to. These animals are completely harmless. In fact, a daddy longlegs won't even try to bite you. The worst thing a daddy longlegs can do to protect itself is give off a bad odor!

True to its name, the daddy longlegs (or harvestman), has very long legs. With such a small body and skinny, sticklike legs, this is truly an odd-looking creature.

What do you suppose a daddy longlegs eats? If you guessed small insects, you are right. You may be surprised that it also eats fruit that it finds on the ground.

So, the next time you find a daddy longlegs, don't forget to be careful as you take it outside! For although it could never harm you, you might accidentally hurt this frail and gentle animal with the funny name.

---

1. A daddy longlegs is

   an insect.   **a spider.**   **neither an insect nor a spider.**

2. Name two things a daddy longlegs eats. _____

3. A good way to describe a daddy longlegs would be

   small and dangerous.

   harmless and fragile.

   long-legged and biting.

Name _____

4. Write about the one way a daddy longlegs can protect itself. _____
    _____

5. What is it about a daddy longlegs that makes it look odd? _____
    _____

6. The animal in this selection has another name besides daddy longlegs. What is it?
    _____

7. Circle the best answer. A legend people tell about the daddy longlegs is that

    it is bad luck to kill one.

    it is good luck to have one in your house.

    it can be a very good pet.

8. Is it safe to pick this creature up with your bare hands? Why or why not? _____
    _____

9. Why should you be careful when taking a daddy longlegs outside? _____
    _____

10. List six words from the story that describe the daddy longlegs.

    _____   _____

    _____   _____

    _____   _____

11. List things that are dangerous to daddy longlegs in woods. _____
    _____

12. Make a list of as many spiders as you can. Circle one and write three facts about it.
    _____
    _____
    _____

Try This!

- Write a story explaining how the daddy longlegs got its strange name. Illustrate your story.
- Write a letter trying to get your parents to let a daddy longlegs live in your house. Be sure to include all the good things you know about this animal.

How Are Fossils Made?

Name _____

Fossils help us learn about plants and animals that no longer live on Earth. For example, we know how many of the dinosaurs looked even though we have never seen any that are alive.

Most plants and animals die and then waste away leaving no clues that they were ever alive. Fortunately, some leave fossils for us to study. Fossils are made in different ways. One kind of fossil is called a *print*. A print forms if the plant or animal dies in soft sand or mud. As the animal wastes away, it leaves an outline in the sand or mud. The sand or mud hardens into rock. The print lets us know exactly how its outline looked.

Another kind of fossil is called a *mold*. This kind of fossil is made from an animal's bones. The bones are buried in matter that will turn to stone someday. Years later, as water begins to seep into the stone, the water carries away tiny parts of the animal and leaves a shape, or mold, inside the rock. This mold can help make a kind of fossil called a *cast.* The water that took away the animal parts also carries minerals. Some of the minerals stay in the mold and get hard. This makes a copy, or cast, of the bone that had been there long ago!

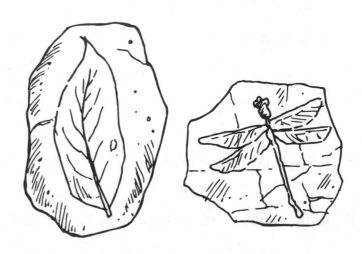

It's a good thing we have fossils. They help us learn about interesting plants and animals that lived long ago.

1. Put a number in front of each sentence to tell the order in which a fossil print is made.

   _____ **The soft material turns to stone.**

   _____ **A plant or animal dies in soft material, such as mud or sand.**

   _____ **The plant or animal wastes away, leaving an outline of the animal or plant.**

FS-30023 Reading Comprehension

Name _____

2. Put a number in front of each sentence to show the correct order in which a mold is made.

_____ **An animal dies.**

_____ **Water carries away the animal parts, little by little.**

_____ **The matter covering the body turns to stone.**

_____ **Water seeps into the stone covering the animal's body.**

_____ **The animal's body is buried in matter.**

3. To make a cast, certain actions must occur. Put a number in front of each sentence to show the correct order in which a cast is made.

_____ **The shape of the animal makes a mold.**

_____ **The hard minerals make a copy of the animal part that was there long ago.**

_____ **Some of the minerals that were in the water stay in the mold.**

_____ **Water with minerals seeps through the mold.**

_____ **Minerals in the mold get hard.**

4. Underline the kind of fossil that was mentioned first in this story.

cast   **mold**   **print**

5. Circle the kind of fossil that was mentioned last in this story.

print   **mold**   **cast**

6. Put a rectangle around the kind of fossil that was mentioned second in the story.

mold   **print**   **cast**

7. What kinds of things have fossils helped us learn about? _____

_____

_____

Try This!

- Go to the library and find out how to make a mold and a cast in order to make a fossil of a chicken bone. In your own words, write the steps involved in order so that a friend can follow your directions.
- Research other kinds of fossils, including petrified bones or plants. Write a paragraph explaining how one of these fossils forms. Remember to write the steps involved in order.

The Computer Craze

Name _____

Computers are everywhere these days. Cash registers in stores, calculators in schools, and even home computers are important parts of our lives. It seems as if we can't live without them. But of course, many years ago, we did.

When do you think the first computer was invented? The answer may surprise you. As early as 1642, over 350 years ago, a computer that only added and subtracted was invented by a man named Blaise Pascal. In 1670, Gottfried von Leibniz of Germany came up with one that would also multiply and divide.

In 1890, the computer proved how useful it could be. Herman Hollerith made a machine that could figure the results of the U.S. census. The census asked millions of people questions about their lives. Hollerith's computer put all the answers together so that, for example, we would know how many Americans in 1890 were women. It was an amazing amount of work. However, 56 of these new computers could put together the results from 6 million people in one day!

In 1939, a computer was made for scientists and engineers. Then, in 1946, the first computer that could be used for many different things was created. It was huge! It weighed 30 tons and took up the same space as a medium-size house!

It was 1975 when the first personal computer (p.c.) was sold. Not many people bought it, but when Apple Computer Company was started in 1977, the Apple p.c. took off! Computers have come a long way since 1642. Aren't you glad?

---

1. Circle which of the three different kinds of computers listed below was invented first.

   a computer for scientists and engineers

   the first personal computer

   the first computer that could be used for many different purposes

The Computer Craze

Name _____

2. Number the following events in the order in which they happened in the story.

____ **A computer for scientists and engineers was invented.**

____ **The Apple Computer Company was started.**

____ **Blaine Pascal invented a machine that could add and subtract.**

____ **An enormous computer that could be used for many things was made.**

____ **Gottfried von Leibniz created a machine that could also multiply and divide.**

____ **The first personal computer was sold.**

____ **The 1890 U.S. census results were figured using Herman Hollerith's computer.**

3. Write one difference between a personal computer and the first computer that could be used for many different purposes. _____

_____

4. List as many places as you can where you see computers daily. _____

_____

_____

5. Write how many years ago the first computer was invented. _____

6. Write what your life would be like today without the computer. _____

_____

_____

_____

7. Write the main idea of this story. _____

_____

8. On the back of this page, draw a picture of a computer you created. Write what it can do.

Try This!

- Computers have gotten better and better over time. Predict what computers will be like in 20 years.
- Look up the history of Apple Computer Company. Compare Apple in 1977 with the same company right now. How did it become so successful?

A Big, Hairy Spider

Name _____

A tarantula is a big, hairy spider. You might have seen one in a pet shop that carries spiders and other unusual pets. In our country, tarantulas live in the west, where it is hot and dry. During the day, tarantulas sleep in holes and other dark places. They come out at night to hunt for food.

Tarantulas catch their food mostly by jumping on it and biting it. Smaller tarantulas eat insects. Larger ones eat mice and lizards. A tarantula's poison can kill the animals it hunts, but its poison cannot kill a human. If you are bitten, you will soon know that a tarantula bite hurts only about as much as a bee sting. Its bite helps this spider protect itself. Tarantulas are shy spiders. They bite humans only if they feel threatened and cannot get away.

A tarantula has another way to protect itself. It can rub its hind legs together which causes its stiff little leg hairs to fly up in the air. Each tiny hair can make a hurtful skin or eye wound.

The tarantula got its name from a big wolf spider that lives near Taranto, Italy. This wolf spider looks similar to tarantulas. People in Taranto used to think that anyone bitten by the wolf spider would get a disease called tarantism. They claimed that a person with that disease would jump in the air and make loud noises. Today, we know this story is untrue. We also know that tarantulas are not the same as wolf spiders.

Circle the best answer based on information you learned from the story.

1. If you visit a pet shop that carries unusual pets, you might see a

    cat.   **puppy.**   **tarantula.**   **canary.**

2. Poking or touching a tarantula might make it

    run away.   **bite you.**   **run after you until it catches you.**

3. Someone who has been bitten by a tarantula will

    jump up in the air, dance, and scream.   **feel a bite like a bee sting.**

Name _____

Fill in the blanks with what you think would happen, based on information in the story.

4. If a lizard stopped near a dark hole at night in the desert, what might happen? _____
_____
_____

5. Explain two things that might happen if a person picked up a tarantula.

   a. _____

   b. _____

6. What might you see if you were to carefully check a hole or other dark place in a desert?_____
_____

7. Someone who reaches carelessly into a hole or under a rock might _____
_____.

8. If you took a tarantula home, what might happen? _____
_____

9. Like you, tarantulas need food each day, and they eat only certain things. If you could not find the right food for a pet tarantula, what would probably happen?
_____

10. If you got down on your knees to look closely at a tarantula that was rubbing its hind legs together, what might happen? _____
_____
_____

11. Write from where the tarantula got its name. _____
_____

12. Write a definition for tarantism. _____
_____

Try This!

- Learn more about tarantulas at the library. Make a list of foods you would have to give a pet tarantula each day to keep it alive. Decide if you could keep a tarantula alive.
- Research to find out more about tarantulas in South America. How are they different from those found in our country?

Quanah Parker, Comanche Chief

Name _____

In 1845, in a part of Texas near a place that is now called Lubbock, a son was born into a Native American tribe called the Comanches. His parents, the Comanche chief Nokoni and his wife, Cynthia Ann Parker, named their son Quanah, which means *fragrant.*

As an adult, Quanah became chief of the Comanches. He worked hard to keep the white settlers from taking advantage of his people. He accomplished a lot, but he was fighting a losing battle.

One thing Quanah did to help the Comanches was to encourage them to get an education and learn to farm their own land. He was able to get many of his tribe members to ask the white settlers to pay for using land that belonged to the Comanches. Quanah was the first Native American chief to get U.S. citizenship for his whole tribe.

Quanah Parker tried to get the white people who were moving into Texas to stop killing the buffalo, but he had to give up that fight in 1875. Still, he had won the respect of many people, whites and Native Americans both.

If you ever go to Texas, be sure to visit a town called Quanah to learn more about this interesting man!

---

1. A good way to describe Quanah Parker would be to say that he

   was afraid to face the white settlers.

   was more interested in saving the buffalo than in saving his people.

   was brave and smart.

   let the white settlers take over the Comanches' land.

Name _____

2. Which of the following would be a good replacement for the title of this story?

    Quanah Parker, Friend to the Buffalo

    Quanah Parker, White Settler and Farmer

    Quanah Parker, Comanche Hero

3. Give three reasons, taken from the story, that show why the title you underlined is a good choice. _____

    _____

    _____

    _____

4. People respected Quanah Parker because_____

    _____

    _____.

5. Tell about one thing Quanah Parker tried to do, but couldn't. _____

    _____

    _____

6. How did Quanah Parker feel about his people? _____

    _____

7. Using the information you read in the story, how do you know he felt that way?

    _____

    _____

8. Write why you think Parker was fighting a losing battle when it came to protecting his people's land from the settlers? _____

    _____

    _____

Try This!

- Look up information on Chief Joseph of the Nez Percé tribe. How was he like Quanah Parker? How were the two leaders different?
- Why did Quanah Parker have to give up on his fight to get white settlers to stop killing buffalo? Find out and add that information to this story. Were there any white settlers on Parker's side helping him with his battle?

The Lone Eagle

Name _____

Today, airplanes fly across oceans every day. Once, this was not true. To go up in an airplane seemed dangerous. Still, a small group of people wanted to fly more than anything else. Charles Lindbergh was one of those people.

As a small boy, Lindbergh loved machinery. As a teenager, he loved a special kind of machinery—airplanes. Lindbergh quit college to fly in air shows and at county fairs. He did tricks in the air with his plane, like flying upside down and in big loops. He traveled from place to place, across the country—a kind of life called barnstorming.

By 1919, no one had flown alone across the Atlantic Ocean. It was still a risky thing to do, and the trip would take many hours. There would be no chance to sleep during the whole trip, and there would be no place to land if the plane had trouble. Raymond Orteig, a hotel owner, offered anyone who made the nonstop trip $25,000! The money was called the Orteig prize after the man who offered it.

By 1927, no one had claimed the Orteig prize, and Lindbergh decided to try. He helped design his plane and called it the "Spirit of St. Louis" after the town his friends came from. Those friends knew Lindbergh was careful, never gave up, and usually succeeded at what he tried, so they helped him pay for the plane. After practicing long flights, Lindbergh took off from a small airfield in New York at 7:52 a.m. on May 20. He took along food and extra gasoline, but no other people were on his plane. On May 21, after a flight that lasted 33 and a half hours, he landed in Paris, France! People around the world respected him for his daring feat and called him "Lucky Lindy" or the "Lone Eagle."

---

1. Lindbergh's friends probably helped pay for his airplane because

   Lindbergh was a wild and daring pilot.

   Lindbergh was nice and could not pay for the plane.

   Lindbergh was a careful pilot and would probably succeed.

FS-30023 Reading Comprehension

The Lone Eagle

Name _____

2. From what you read in the story, you know that Lindbergh was

    courageous.   **dumb.**   **happy.**   **sad.**

3. Which one of Lindbergh's character traits might have helped him the most when he flew across the Atlantic alone? _____

4. People often described Lindbergh as *daring.* In your own words, what does *daring* mean? _____

    _____

5. People called Lindbergh "Lucky Lindy." Do you think luck had much to do with his safe flight from New York to Paris? Explain why or why not. _____

    _____

    _____

6. From what you know about Charles Lindbergh, which nickname do you think fits him best, "Lucky Lindy" or the "Lone Eagle?"_____

    Explain your answer. _____

    _____

    _____

7. Raymond Orteig offered money to anyone who could make this dangerous flight. What do you think he was like and why? _____

    _____

    _____

8. It is probably not surprising that Lindbergh loved airplanes because as a small boy,

    _____

9. In your own words, write a definition for *barnstorming.* _____

    _____

Try This!

- Read a book about Charles Lindbergh. List his character traits as you discover them in the book.
- Make up a new nickname for Charles Lindbergh that will explain what kind of a person he was.

The Black Widow

Name _____

We all jump back when we see a spider nearby, even though most spiders are perfectly harmless. Still, no matter how much you may like spiders, or find them interesting, take a good look before you reach out to help one return to its home outside. Is it black? If it is, it may be a black widow—the most dangerous spider in the United States.

Chances are you will only meet a black widow if you go into a dark corner of your attic or garage. These spiders are only awake at night, and they prefer dark places. Be careful! A shoe that is left in a garage at night can become the perfect home for a black widow.

A black widow's bite injects poison into your body. This poison causes terrible pain in the person bitten, sometimes for days, or even weeks. Fortunately, the only time this spider will bite is in self-defense. For that reason, you need to be especially careful in places like sheds and garages. Always look carefully before you reach your hand or foot into any box or dark area of the building.

Most black widows live in the southern part of the United States, but they have been found in most of the states, as well as in Canada. Just to be on the safe side, keep your eyes open for shiny black spiders living in messy-looking webs, and keep your hands and feet out of dark corners and boxes!

_____

1. You might meet a black widow if _____

_____ or if

_____ .

2. If you leave your shoe outside or in the garage, _____

_____ .

Name _____

3. A black widow will only bite you

   if it feels it needs to defend itself.

   if you are moving too quickly.

   if it sees you.

   if it can get close enough to you.

4. What will a black widow's poison do to you if you are bitten? _____
_____

5. You should be especially careful in places like sheds and garages because _____
_____.

6. You should take a good look before you reach out to help a spider return to its home outside because

   the spider might be a black widow.

   the spider might be an especially pretty one.

   you might find a better place to put the spider.

   it might be a spider you have seen before.

7. In the last paragraph of the story, it says to "keep your eyes open for shiny black spiders living in messy-looking webs." Why? _____
_____

8. List places that make good homes for black widows. _____
_____

9. Write why you would not like to get bitten by a black widow. _____
_____

Try This!

- Every female black widow spider has a special mark that will help you to identify her. Find out what it is and draw a picture of it.
- Pretend you are a black widow. Write a story about one day in your life as a spider. Be sure to include where you live, what you do at night, and what you like to eat.

Where Did the Dinosaurs Go?

Name _____

All dinosaurs died many, many years ago, before humans began to walk on Earth. What happened to them? No one knows for sure. Once, though, dinosaurs lived all over Earth. Then, suddenly they were all gone. Because there are no dinosaurs alive, scientists study the fossils of plants and animals to try to discover what might have happened to them. Scientists have many ideas about what caused dinosaurs to die out, but no one can absolutely prove their ideas.

Some scientists believe the cooler climate of the Cretaceous Period caused the dinosaurs to die. These scientists have studied crocodiles and turtles and other living animals that may be related to dinosaurs. They discovered that if the weather gets much hotter or much cooler than usual, all of these babies are either boys, or they are all girls. If that happened over a long period of time, there could be no babies. That would cause all dinosaurs to disappear.

Other scientists believe an asteroid hit the Earth and caused the deaths of all dinosaurs. Asteroids are like small planets. If one had hit Earth, it would have caused a lot of dust to fly up high into the atmosphere. The heat from the asteroid crash would have caused huge, smoky fires. So much dust and smoke would have blocked the heat and light from the sun. If the sun's rays had been blocked, plants would have died. If the plants had died, all of the animals that ate only plants would have died, too. When the plants and plant-eaters had died, the animals that ate mainly meat would have starved and died, too. Soon, there would have been no dinosaurs.

1. We can be sure that all dinosaurs died long ago because

   scientists study crocodiles.

   there are no dinosaurs left on Earth.

2. The cooler climate of the Cretaceous Period might have caused

   fewer dinosaurs to hatch.

   all dinosaur babies to be either girls or boys.

   dinosaurs to freeze to death.

Where Did the Dinosaurs Go?

Name _____

Complete these sentences.

3. Some people think the cooler climate of the Cretaceous Period caused _____

   _____

4. If an asteroid crashed into Earth, the sun's rays might have been blocked because

   _____

5. Why would plants have died if there had been dark smoke and dust in the

   atmosphere? _____

   _____

6. Scientists believe plant-eating dinosaurs died first if an asteroid hit the Earth. Why?

   _____

   _____

7. If all of the plants died, why would meat-eating dinosaurs die, too? _____

   _____

   _____

8. Scientists cannot agree about why dinosaurs died. Which of the two reasons given in

   the story do you believe? _____

   _____

   Why do you think that reason is the most likely?_____

   _____

   _____

9. Write the names of animals some scientists believe dinosaurs were related to.

   _____

10. On the back of this page, write something you can do to prevent one other endangered
    animal from becoming extinct.

Try This!

- Research to learn about other ideas people have concerning the fate of
  dinosaurs. Decide which you believe is true. Write two paragraphs
  explaining this idea and why it makes the most sense to you.
- Make a comic strip showing what you think happened to the dinosaurs.
  Show it to a classmate and explain your ideas.

A Visit to the Doctor

Name _____

They both start with a rash on your skin, but they are very different illnesses. Can you guess which conditions these are? You may or may not have had chickenpox or measles, but surely you've heard of them. Below are some ways your doctor uses to tell them apart and treat them.

Chickenpox is a mild illness that starts with a skin rash and a low fever. People who catch this disease often have a headache and usually don't feel good all over. The rash is itchy. Soon the rash turns into bumps, which show up on the skin in groups, and turn into blisters. The blisters may become filled with a milky liquid before turning into scabs.

Chickenpox, which is caused by a virus, is catching, but if you've already had it, you probably won't get it again. If you have chickenpox, your doctor will offer some ways to stop the itching. Some of these ways include taking oatmeal baths and applying anti-itching lotion. Most people who get chickenpox are children.

Measles is a serious illness that spreads easily from person to person. The first signs of measles are a fever, which can sometimes go as high as 105 degrees, red and watery eyes, a cough, and a runny nose. Small pink spots with grayish-white centers usually develop inside the mouth and on the insides of the cheeks. Several days later, the rash spreads all over the body.

A virus causes measles, which occurs mostly in children. In most cases, a person will only have measles once. Nowadays, however, if you take a measles shot, you will most likely never have this illness. Before the 1960's, most children in the U.S. caught measles. But thanks to a team of doctors, a measles vaccine was developed in 1963. By 1982, measles had almost been wiped out of the U.S.

---

1. Measles and chickenpox are both

   serious.   **hard to cure.**   **viruses.**

2. Two uncomfortable problems that happens in both illnesses are _____

   _____.

FS-30023 Reading Comprehension

A Visit to the Doctor

Name _____

3. Most people who get chickenpox are   **adults.**   **children.**

4. Most people who get measles are   **adults.**   **children.**

5. Write a **T** for True or an **F** for False.

___ **Both measles and chickenpox occur mostly in children.**

___ **You can't get a shot to keep from getting measles.**

___ **The skin rash bumps occur in groups for both measles and chickenpox.**

___ **If you get either measles or chickenpox once, you probably won't get it again.**

___ **Measles is a more serious sickness than chickenpox.**

___ **A person with measles will cough and have a runny nose, unlike a person who has chickenpox.**

6. Write two things measles and chickenpox have in common. _____

_____

_____

7. Tell about one difference._____

_____

_____

8. Find two words in the story that mean *eliminated.* _____

9. List in order the signs that tell you that you have measles. _____

_____

_____

10. Write one word from the story that means *contagious.* _____

Try This!

• Make up a new illness. Give it a name. Tell what signs show up in a person who has it. How long does it last? Is it mild or serious? Who mostly gets it?

• If you have had measles or chickenpox, write about your experience. If you haven't had either one, ask someone who has to tell you all about it. Then write about it as if it were your experience. How did it start? How did it feel? How long did it last? How did you know you had it, and how did you know what it was?

FS-30023 Reading Comprehension

Horns or Antlers?

Name _____

Horns and antlers are different in some ways and the same in others. Can you tell the difference? Deer are the only animals with antlers, and there are about 60 kinds of deer around the world, including moose, elk, caribou, reindeer, and musk deer. Many kinds of animals have horns including antelope, cattle, goats, and sheep. Both horns and antlers grow from the top of an animal's head. Animals that have antlers and horns use them to defend themselves. Males with horns or antlers use them to prove which male in the group is strongest.

So, what's the difference between horns and antlers? Horns are made of bone covered with a hard material, much like your fingernails, only much thicker. Horns can be curved or straight, but each horn is only one piece. A horn never branches. Many horns have a sharp point at the end, which helps an animal use it as a weapon. Think about the horns of a longhorn bull. These horns would help an animal fight off a wolf or a coyote or other hunting animal.

Antlers differ from horns both inside and out! Antlers form branches on a deer's head. Older deer can have many branches on their antlers. A deer first begins to grow its antlers in the summer when it is a year or two old. Antlers always fall off in late winter. Horns never fall off. Antlers are made up of layers of soft tissue that later harden. The soft, hairy skin on the outside of antlers looks like velvet. It hardens by fall, at which time the deer scrapes it off. Horns do not have a soft covering at any time of the year. Now when you look at an animal that has "headgear," do you think you can tell whether it has horns or antlers?

_____

1. In the story, underline each feature that relates only to horns.

2. Put a circle around each feature that belongs only to antlers.

3. All animals that have horns or antlers use them for _____.

Name _____

4. Write where horns and antlers grow on animals. _____

_____

5. It has branches.   **horns**   **antlers**   **antlers and horns**

6. The center of this headgear is bone, and the outside is like your fingernails.

    horns   **antlers**   **antlers and horns**

7. Males use these to prove which is the strongest in their group.

    horns   **antlers**   **antlers and horns**

8. Only a deer can grow this on its head.   **horns**   **antlers**   **antlers and horns**

9. A soft, hairy skin that looks like velvet grows on these.

    horns   **antlers**   **antlers and horns**

10. These can be used as weapons.   **horns**   **antlers**   **antlers and horns**

11. Use a red pencil to make a box around each word in the story that names a kind of animal that has antlers.

12. Use a blue pencil to make a box around each word in the story that names a kind of animal that has horns.

13. Only one kind of animal can grow antlers. What is it? _____

14. A verb is an action word. Find 10 verbs in the story. Write them on these lines. _____

_____

15. A compound word is made of two words. Find three compound words in the story and write them on these lines. _____

16. A noun is a person, place, or thing. List 10 nouns from the story on these lines. ____

_____

17. How many words in the story name kinds of deer? _____

18. Write them on these lines. _____

_____

Try This!

- Make a crossword puzzle with sentences that explain the differences between horns and antlers.
- Read books about different kinds of deer at the library. Write a book of your own telling about two kinds that you learned about.

FS-30023 Reading Comprehension

The Grocer's Daughter

Name _____

Margaret Thatcher was born in 1925 in Great Britain. About 54 years later, she became the first woman prime minister of her country and the first woman leader of a major western nation. While she grew up, Margaret's family lived above the grocery store they owned and operated. Maggie, as she was called, often worked in the store. She liked listening to her father talk with people who came to shop. Maggie's father was a part of the town government. People talked to him about politics, or ways to run the government.

As a young girl, Maggie liked to do her best and to win at any contest she entered. She was an excellent student and the youngest captain of her school hockey team. She did so well at her studies that she was accepted at Oxford University, one of the world's best, where she studied chemistry. "I am a born hard worker," she said. "I watched my mother work like a Trojan in the shop and home."

Maggie was 23 when she ran for office the first time. She lost, but she continued to run for office at other elections. She was first elected to a government office in 1959 when she was 33. In that job, she helped make laws for her country. During this time, her country had many problems. Maggie Thatcher believed a strong leader and new ideas could help. Many others thought Maggie was strong enough to do the job. Some called her the Iron Lady. This didn't upset Maggie. She said, "Any leader has to have a certain amount of steel in them, so I am not that put out about being called the Iron Lady." Maggie Thatcher ran for office as political leader of her country and was elected to two terms. During that time, she worked to solve some of her country's problems and became a respected world leader.

---

1. From the story, you can tell something about Maggie Thatcher's personality. Circle the words below that you believe best describe her.

   shy   **strong**   **lazy**   **boring**   **hard-working**

Put a √ next to the sentence you believe is most correct.

2. Maggie probably liked listening to her father talk because

   ___ **she wanted to learn about politics.**

   ___ **she wanted an excuse to get out of work.**

   ___ **her dad told her it was good for her.**

Name _____

3. Maggie probably got into Oxford University because

___ **she was a girl.**

___ **she worked very hard to get there.**

___ **it was easy to get into that school.**

4. Because she lost her first election but kept on trying, we can tell that

___ **Maggie did not give up easily.**

___ **Maggie was really not good at running for office.**

___ **she gave up easily.**

5. Some people call Maggie Thatcher the Iron Lady because

___ **she wears iron jewelry.**

___ **she likes to iron.**

___ **she is tough.**

6. Maggie thought a strong leader could help her country. She probably ran for that office because

___ **she believed she was strong enough to do the job.**

___ **no one else in her country would run for that office.**

___ **she was sure she could have fun doing the job.**

7. Maggie Thatcher was the first woman prime minister of her country. She was probably elected because

___ **only women voted for her in that election.**

___ **so many people thought she could do the job.**

___ **no men voted in the election.**

8. Why do you think Maggie was not upset about being called the Iron Lady?

_____

_____

Try This! Research to find out about another woman who has become the head of her country. Write a paragraph that explains how you know she was a good or bad leader from what you read.

Cactus Survival Tips

Name _____

If you've ever been in a desert, you know it isn't an easy place in which to live. How does a cactus do it? If you had the right body parts, you could, too!

One important part a cactus has is its long roots. They don't go far underground, but they stretch out quite far just under the surface. That way, when it rains, the cactus can collect as much water as possible to keep for later use.

The stem of a cactus also helps it to survive by storing water for the cactus. Because the skin of the cactus is so waxy, the water does not evaporate, but rather stays inside the cactus to be used as it is needed.

Most cacti have spines to keep from being eaten by animals. The spines grow out of lumps in the stem. In some cactuses, these lumps line up to make ribs. A cactus that has ribs enjoys some shade; its ribs also help it to keep water.

Do you have any of these body parts? If you don't, and you're planning on living out in the open desert, you may want to take some survival tips from the cactus: store water and protect your skin! Who could give you better advice?

---

1. Using a pencil, underline the name of the place in which most cactuses live wherever you see it in the selection.

2. Use a red marker or crayon to circle the parts of a cactus that help it store water.

3. Draw a box around each verb that you find in the story.

4. Find a word in the story that means "to change into a gas or vapor." Write it on the line.

   _____

5. Use a yellow crayon or marker to highlight an adjective that describes the skin of the cactus.

6. Draw a zigzag line under any interrogative sentences in the story.

7. Draw an X on top of any exclamations in the story.

8. On the line below, write any contractions you find in the story.

   _____

Answers

Pages 2 and 3

1. The Roosevelt children had fun while living in the White House.
2. The White House gang got into mischief in the White House.
3. Answers will vary.
4. One child rode a pony upstairs. The children spit paper balls at Andrew Jackson's picture. They declared war on the White House.

5-6. Answers will vary.

7. parrot, bear, lizard, rooster, barn owl, rabbit, pig, pony
8. Answers will vary.
9. He asked for peace through his war department.

10.-12. Answers will vary.

Pages 4 and 5

1. Dian Fossey studied and taught other people about mountain gorillas.
2. She wrote a book about them.
3. She copied their habits and sounds.
4. Hunters were killing the gorillas.
5. read a book about them.
6. Fossey taught the world about mountain gorillas and worked hard to save them.

7.-9. Answers will vary.

Pages 6 and 7

1. Answers will vary.
2. Teddy Roosevelt, 42
3. James Madison, our fourth president, was the shortest president we have had so far. He was 5-feet-4-inches tall. Six-foot-four-inch Abraham Lincoln was the tallest, and he was also very thin. William Howard Taft, our 27th president, was the heaviest. He weighed more than 300 pounds and even got stuck in the White House bathtub the first time he used it!
4. three
5. The youngest man to become

president was 42-year-old Teddy Roosevelt, who became our 26th president. John F. Kennedy was also a young president. He was 43 when he was elected our 35th president in 1960. three

6. Teddy Roosevelt's children had a pony named Algonquin, and John Kennedy's children had a pony named Macaroni! one
7. a. Abraham Lincoln d. Teddy Roosevelt c. William Taft
8. two
9. William Howard Taft got stuck in the bathtub the first time he used it in the White House. Millard Fillmore put the first bathtub in the White House.
10. Both were young when they became president. Both brought young children to the White House. The children of each of these presidents had a pony.
11. Teddy Roosevelt was 42, JFK was 43; TR, the 26th president, JFK, the 35th president; TR's pony was named Algonquin, and JFK's pony was named Macaroni.
12. James Madison
13. 5'4"
14. 6'4"
15. Abe Lincoln
16. Answers will vary.

Pages 8 and 9

1. neither an insect nor a spider.
2. insects, fruit
3. harmless and fragile.
4. It can give off a bad smell.
5. It has a small body compared to its long legs.
6. harvestman
7. it is bad luck to kill one.
8. It is safe, because a daddy longlegs is harmless.
9. It is frail, and you may accidentally hurt it.
10. harmless, odd-looking, small, skinny, gentle, frail

11.-12. Answers will vary.

Pages 10 and 11

1. 3, 1, 2
2. 1, 5, 3, 4, 2
3. 1, 5, 3, 2, 4
4. print
5. cast
6. mold
7. Answers will vary but should include something about helping us learn about plants and animals that no longer live on Earth.

Pages 12 and 13

1. a computer for scientists and engineers
2. 4, 7, 1, 5, 2, 6, 3
3. A personal computer is much smaller.

4.-6. Answers will vary.

7. Computers are everywhere these days.
8. Answers will vary.

Pages 14 and 15

1. tarantula.
2. bite you.
3. feel a bite like a bee sting.
4. A tarantula might jump on it, bite it, and eat it.
5. A person might get bitten; a person might get tiny tarantula hairs in his or her skin or eyes.
6. a tarantula
7. get bitten by a tarantula.
8. Answers will vary.
9. It might die.
10. You might get tarantula hairs in your eyes or in other parts of your body; or you might get bitten.
11. The tarantula got its name from a big wolf spider that lives near Taranto, Italy.
12. A disease contracted from the wolf spider that makes a person jump in the air and make loud noises.

Answers

Pages 16 and 17

1. was brave and smart.
2. Quanah Parker, Comanche Hero
3.-4. Answers will vary.
5. He couldn't keep the white settlers from killing the buffalo.
6. Answer should include Parker's positive feelings about his people.
7.-8. Answers will vary.

Pages 18 and 19

1. Lindbergh was a careful pilot and would probably succeed.
2. courageous.
3.-7. Answers will vary.
8. he loved machinery.
9. To appear, as at fairs, in exhibitions of stunt flying and parachute jumping

Pages 20 and 21

1. you go into a dark corner of your attic or garage; you are out in your yard at night.
2. it may become a black widow's home.
3. if it feels it needs to defend itself.
4. It will cause terrible pain.
5. if you reach your hand or foot into a box or dark area without looking, the spider may bite in self-defense.
6. the spider might be a black widow.
7. There may be a black widow living there.
8. attics, garages, sheds, yards, boxes, shoes
9. Answers will vary.

Pages 22 and 23

1. there are no dinosaurs left on Earth.
2. all dinosaur babies to be either girls or boys.
3. all dinosaurs to die out after all boy or all girl dinosaurs hatched.
4. of the dust and smoke in the air.

5. They need the sun's heat and light to grow.
6. Plants died from the lack of sunlight and heat.
7. Because they ate plant-eating dinosaurs, which died after there were no more plants. No more food was left for either kind of dinosaur.
8. Answers will vary.
9. crocodiles and turtles
10. Answers will vary.

Pages 24 and 25

1. viruses.
2. fever, itchy skin rash
3. children
4. children
5. T, F, F, T, T, T
6.- 7. Answers will vary.
8. wiped out
9. rash, fever, red, watery eyes, cough, and runny nose
10. catching

Pages 26 and 27

1. Horns are made of bone covered with a hard material; Horns can be curved or straight, but each horn is only one piece. A horn never branches. Many horns have a sharp point at the end, which helps an animal use it as a weapon.
2. Antlers form branches on a deer's head. Older deer can have many branches on their antlers. A deer first begins to grow its antlers when it is a year or two old. Antlers always fall off in late winter. Antlers are made up of layers of soft tissue that later harden. The soft, hairy skin on the outside of antlers looks like velvet. It hardens by fall, at which time the deer scrapes it off.
3. defense
4. from the top of an animal's head
5. antlers

6. horns
7. antlers and horns
8. antlers
9. antlers
10. antlers and horns
11. deer, moose, elk, caribou, reindeer, musk deer
12. antelope, cattle, goats, sheep
13. deer
14.-16. Answers will vary.
17. five
18. moose, elk, caribou, reindeer, musk deer

Pages 28 and 29

1. strong, hard-working
2. she wanted to learn about politics.
3. she worked very hard to get there.
4. Maggie did not give up easily.
5. she is tough.
6. she believed she was strong enough to do the job.
7. so many people thought she could do the job.
8. Answers will vary.

Page 30

1. *Desert* should be underlined.
2. roots, stem, ribs, skin
3. Check students' stories.
4. evaporate
5. waxy
6. Check students' stories.
7. Check students' stories.
8. Check students' stories.

FS-30023 Reading Comprehension